David Rhaesa
655 South Santa Fe
Salina Kansas
67401

Fugitive Histories

to David —
keep well —
Harley Elliott

Woodley Memorial Press

Fugitive Histories

*Poems by
Harley Elliott*

Acknowledgments

Thanks to the readers and editors in whose publications some of these poems first appeared:

> *Cottonwood Review*
> *Hanging Loose*
> *Imagination & Place*
> *The Little Balkans Review*
> *Midwest Quarterly*
> *New Letters*
> *Northeast*
> *Pearl*
> *Raccoon*
> *Stray Dog*

Copyright © 2011 by Harley Elliott

Edited by Kevin Rabas
Published by Woodley Press
Washburn University
Topeka, Kansas 66621
All rights reserved

Printed in the United States of America

First Edition

ISBN 978-0-9828752-0-9
Library of Congress Control Number: 2010943096

for Elaine and Dario

CONTENTS

Around Here
Inconvenient Lives 3
What to Do Around Here 4
Untitled 5
Somewhere In The History Of Tools 6
The Farmer Finds A Bolt 7
Calling Bindweed Pretty 8
Custer In La La Land 9
Hot Pig In Clover 11
Breakfast At Kanopolis Drive-in 12
Dancing With Rattlers 14
To Build A Fence In The Rain 15
One Thing Running Said 16
Walking Like Always 17
A Round For The Sacrificial Pike 18
Found Conversations 20
Front Of The Lodge 22
Dream Lock 23
Guitar 24
Choosing A Way 25
Nature Study 26
A Personal Philosophy 27
My Brother's Theory 29
After The Hunt 30
Ride 31
Behind 32
Kansas Night Storm 33
Journey 34
Connection 35

Ghost World
Starting Point 39
The Invention Of The Doorway 40
The Cherokee Princess Factory 41
Timeless Peasants Report 42
The Skunk 44
Private Property 45
To Recognize Evil 46
Porches And Kitchens 47
Howling For Dollars 48
In Another Life 49
Bird Master 51
At The Stoplight 52
Why You Should Read This Poem 53
Smugglers Of Hammers 54
Moon And Shadow 55
Trouble Brewing As Hogs Near Paradise 56
White Boys In Control 57
Snooker 58
Ghost World 60
Against Surrender 61
Living To Tell About It 62
Just Before Midnight 63
Being New 64
Preparing to Leap To The Moon 65
Dirt 66
Speak Now 68

Around Here

Inconvenient Lives

To say the bottom fell out
of the corn market might
explain it to some
but the woman ringed
by eight children
fed one ear of corn
after another into the
iron stove that winter
the stock market as
mysterious as Dakota wind
and wept at burning
good food cheaper than
wood to keep warm.

Nothing but prairie surrounds
the red-faced man running
over stony ground
knowing even if he reached
somewhere the best would
be too little and the
girl with the rattlesnake bite
going dark in his arms
will not come back.

Those moments long gone
except for me and now you
and we might wonder
in our modern way
What's the problem?
Kill all the rattlesnakes.
Eat all the corn.
Case closed.   But those

were necessary lives
before convenience was exalted
when our grandmothers honored
food with their tears and
against fate our grandfathers
continued to run.

What To Do Around Here

take in a full pink
moonrise over prairie roads
where the strong south wind
smells pale and early blooming

if the moon makes you
walk up the ditch and
put your ear against
a telephone pole
you had better do it

a seven thousand fathom wind
drones in that old wood
deeper than darkening blue
twilight seeping west overhead

say hello to the ghost of birth
and the earth keyed tight
to this ripe blush of spring

just you the moon
and winds voice in the
spine of a tree
you will think something
seems wise about the moment
and you will know it isn't you

Untitled

In shifting leaf shadow
the little bird of
a thousand browns
lifts one white eyebrow.
It comes like

all good education
as a surprise when
being shines through labels.
Wind becomes a color
hard to recognize.

A heartbeat you might
once have called your own
appears without history
or promise in the
eye of a nameless bird.

Somewhere In The History Of Tools

To the beginner it was a friend.

To the man of leisure it was
stereo carpeted air conditioned
icebox full of beer.

To the worms
who dived at its distant vibration
it was the ordained
Changing Of The World.

To the ghost it was a dreadful
ghost loudly dragging
its guts around all afternoon.

To hawks it was the line maker
that flushed crawlers and runners.

To the horse and ox
it was an inside joke.

To the farmer it was the breath
of the bank on his neck.

To the earth it was a
thing that comes and passes
came and passed.

The dirt having seen everything
was moved but not impressed.

The Farmer Finds A Bolt

Dark farm barn and yard
where halogen worklights turn
the dust on one side of
the faded red combine green

mid-harvest
the machine is down.

The farmer's finger
is invested with gravity
as it stirs in a coffee can
looking for the linchpin
to his universe
"write that down" he says
to nothing in particular

"I not only found the
nine sixteenth inch bolt
I also found the nut"
the evidence
cradled into light

the belt will be returned
engine repaired
the towering fat wheel

refitted to its axle
and he can promise wheat
tomorrow he'll be there

worklights pool the prairie
where farmers hang on

their coffee cans full
of assorted bits
of the farms of America
are bringing in the bread.

Calling Bindweed Pretty

can get you educated
fast in these parts
might as well champion
chickenhawks where every
hawk is one or suggest
a charm in snakes

words of vermin or weed
sworn allegiance to
grow outlaws of human domain
an invasive drag
on the plan

ghost prairie dog towns
and every hand
against a coyote
we know what it takes

your little flowered creeper
is pretty all right
but pretty is not on the list
no matter how sweet
the thief may be

Custer In La La Land

He camped once near here
though hard to dazzle
norse and irish farmers did
not put him on the map.

They call the place Big Hill.
It has more trees now
thick flanks of wild plum
tangled oaks that try to
sneak through wind like

Custer on splendid sandstone
sky wide with stars
stars of his flag his country
not the country he belongs to

but the country that belongs to him.
This place that claims
the world's largest prairie dog
deepest hand dug well and
maybe largest ball of twine

does not honor his
philosophical camp on this
peasant of a hill.
His orderly prepares his

writing material so he may rehearse
the day he becomes
leader of all these stars
while pipers strike up Garry Owen.

He will have grown
his hair again for a
golden grateful nation
but in history now here

a windy night on Big Hill
invisible to his dream are others
shifting in the dark.
Custer writes another line.

Hot Pig In Clover

At one hundred ten degrees
the cloverfield sweats aromatic purple.
The grey pig stands snout down
too sunstruck or hypnotized
by bees to care.

Even to look at another
creature is a chore
at one hundred ten degrees
is the thought of the pig
mind yawning with clover vapor.

The humans he thinks
might very well at one hundred
ten degrees drop the big one
seeing himself as a brief
puddle of violet lard.

At one hundred ten motionless
he suddenly perceived the
true nature of existence.
Reality was: a hot pig in clover.
Take me Lord of all

swine he thought
ready now to die and go
down in a sweet cloud of purple.
But one hundred ten degrees is
too hot for remembering.
Soon he was just
another hot pig in clover.

Breakfast At Kanopolis Drive-In

Instead of throwing our
sleeping bags down on any
curving swath of prairie grass
camp could be made at the
tiny Kanopolis Drive-In where
five cars might

show up at dusk to watch
Audie or Randolph or Joel
restrain his moral outrage but
always pushed too far
until the sun came up

dozing and coming back
two of four awake at any
given time for shootouts and
Audie or Randy or Joel pressing
a woman to them with
of course no penetration

while light seeps into the
horizon behind the screen
somebody awake gathers napkins
paper cups dead branches
along the back fence

the people in five cars all
sleep the projectionist sleeps
in an empty gravel space
we make the small fire
for eggs skillet spatula
lard coffee from the trunk

take breakfast while the
west is finally won
moral equilibrium restored

and birds declare the day
the hero waves from a
distant ridge and we wave back

knowing with teenage certainty
we would have shot the villain
in the back first chance
and shoved our hands under
the schoolmarm's many skirts

which is why Audie and Randy
and Joel ride into a
rectangular pretense of sunset
and leave us this borderless
inescapable dawn

Dancing With Rattlers

This wet early spring
rattlesnakes turn in their sleep
and come up clustered on warm rock
velvet tails wideawake
and the diamonds that blur.
Now you whose feet

love the earth too much
snap out and back:
do not stumble through this company.

The ring of rattles is your beat.
If you think of supper or sex
you lose: these masters of the dance
are professional and sincere.

Tapping through rattle
click hop strike cross
glance just ahead of your toes
you know nothing lingers long.

To Build A Fence In The Rain

you need to want the fence
beyond anything.
Time equals wire:
get it strung
get it stretched
get it stuck.

Duckwalking gulley mud
barbs spanging off the roll
for once you don't pick up
every turtle snake or stone.

Fixing metal strand on metal pole
steel pliers pockets full of metal clips
metal stretcher chain dragging wet grass
where you fling it into and lean against
the metal truck   tell me
is the lightning still galloping
off in the southwest?

No matter how hard it rains
shift your noisy boots
and say it's letting up.

One Thing Running Said

To pause is death stranger
they have made me out a hobo
and a network of dogs is out
looking for me

though I ought to tear your
throat out to show you
what it's like to be
mistaken for an enemy

then there were only green
and silver cottonwood trees.

Walking Like Always

That night I drained out
of one world and walked in another
mugged by high noon heat

beside my friend walking like always
a plowed field where arrowheads
made long ago sometimes appear.

When I veer off to rest in
the shade of the old green pickup
he keeps walking but
wait a minute neither of us

owns a green truck and
how come his hair is now
a brilliant silver white.
Now I remember he died
two months and ten days ago.

I will wave him over
next time he wanders close
to ask how he can be here
and is the hot blue sky
as real for him as for me

but he does not wander close
gives only a glimpse
of a one-sided smile
from clear across the field
he can feel me getting it

watching from the shade
of reunion and farewell
while he continues
walking like always.

A Round For The Sacrificial Pike

Meanwhile on top of the water
things are getting hot
for a certain walleyed pike
who hangs quiet in deep green.

Simply by existing
he determines the day
for two thousand sportshumans.
They could have flown to Cairo
slept in walked the dog

but he has brought them here
filling the water with shimmy
and jerk of ersatz fish meal
purple worms and sacred plugs
petition his glory.

He has seen others bite and
do the sudden Up Dive
a phenomenon among fish.
Undulating the red tag in his fin
his knot of a brain
makes no sense of the lake bottom

covered by the human offering
of valuable aluminum cylinders
or the top of his lake crowded
with noise and bobbing ovals.

One day ago he was worth
exactly his weight in protein
today he equals a boat and a trailer.

For his fame   until sundown
this lashing of water.
To him all the ceremonial ale drunk

one torpedo!
two portedo!
three tordepo!
for him the sweaty angler cries.

Green in ignorance
the sacrificial pike just swims
beyond the fever of another species.
Perhaps he will eat.
Perhaps he will not.

Found Conversations

1. Short Reality

Honey I have to go to work.
OK. Goodbye honey.
Boys now I want you to do your mother a big
favor and rake all these leaves out of the kitchen. Well,
I'm going hunting. Hey, there's an eagle.
Have a good day honey.
I'm back and here's the eagle.
Oh good. Just put it in the crock pot.
Wow dad, we want to hunt eagles too.
OK boys.
Goodbye honey.
Look honey, we got eighteen eagles.
And a hawk, mom!
Just put them in the crockpot.
They won't fit, mom.
Just stuff them in there.
They won't fit, mom!
Ok, just lay them down there.
Well, I've got to get back to my hunting.
Ok honey.
Knock, knock, anybody home?
I'll get it mom. Who's there?
It's your cousin Jack. I just got on the train, I mean
I just got in on the train.
Who is it, son?
It's our cousin, mom.
Jack?
Yeah.
OK. Don't walk on the eagles, boys.
OK mom.
Hi Jack, I'm dad. Want to hunt some eagles?
Sure.
Goodbye honey.

2. Tall Reality

Anybody home?
I'll get it. Hi, I'm dad.
I'm Colonel Goodnight from
the eagle ranch down the road
and this is
my daughter, Princessa.
Oh.
Some of our eagles aren't
coming back to roost at night
and we heard you all were
hunters so we thought you
might have seen them . . .
No, no, I didn't see any eagles,
did you, boys?
No, dad.
. . . while you were out hunting?
Well, we don't hunt eagles.
What do you hunt?
Wolves, we hunt wolves.
Yeah, dad, wolves wolves.
Look father! there by the crock pot!
It's Old Baldy!
Not Old Baldy!
That's not our eagle.
What about all those eagles
stuffed in the crock pot?
Those ain't our eagles, either.
You boys know anything
about those eagles?
No, dad.
That's not even
our crock pot, dad.

Front Of The Lodge

At that center any morning
each breath cloudy silence
whether ice or a sun
hurries to power

a woodpecker face considers
from a circle in a tree
the language of crows
or the shadows of crows

in the driveway rut
a blackbird wades in the sky
bends and drinks
a drop of water

falls to the sky
repeats itself in all directions
a force beyond self
the day takes on a name

Dream Lock

Cast up against my front door
late at night   the lock
works hard   the sound of tumblers
clacking into place
a key to dreams.

At two years old you were
learning how to talk:
I was learning what to say.
The lock snaps open
you are running and
calling one word

lifting me then and even
now in this dark
house far away
lifting me out of my moonlit shoes.

Guitar

Don't be caught in any company
saying a guitar is
like a woman
and if you find

your guitar is like a woman
get rid of it.
Find one like no thing.

Charles Darwin looked at the mud
from the claw of a partridge
and identified eighty two seeds.
He did not think
a guitar was like a woman.

He was busy hearing
the music of the glacier
and refrained throughout
from turning women into guitars

and as you draw
your hand across these strings
so my son should we.

Choosing A Way

On his promise to return
Joe Red Hawk was allowed
to ride with his teacher
and a visiting poet
from the penitentiary

where he lived for
getting drunk and killing
an old man
to a college to stand
and read his poetry.

He who in solitude looked
far down the dead end
found a strange true voice
lowered his head to applause
and afterward requested
cigarettes to take back.

When the teacher left that
car to buy your smokes
time pivots Joe Red Hawk
and thirty years gone
your way still lives
sitting in a parking lot

thinking of flight
and only a poet between
you and the sky
but now your word
is your freedom.

Nature Study

Couple old guys carping
at their sons   dammit boys
don't run through that wet grass.
Trying to keep camp fire
alive in hot noon rain.

Sons hurl themselves at the day.
Every hair sweats. Every snake
in the field disappears.

Old guys get the canoe in the water
where tall poles topped with wooden wheels
dangle catfish heads.
Yes boys   it's the Catfish
Decapitation Virility Syndrome.
Well boys have seen better

gothic parable on television.
Far more exciting the yellow plastic
newspaper wrappers snagged in roots
the canoe glides by.

Couple old guys point out
duck with blue wings
rushing her fat kids into weeds.
Flopping around the bend
she performs classical O Dear.

Seven tangled wrappers pass
before she takes flight squanking:
another tub of humans outmaneuvered.

Old guys seeing lessons
yes boys   lessons
sons see plastic   water
sky   blue wing   duck
endless possibility.

A Personal Philosophy

"Excuse me mister"
I could not say at
the age of ten
"but you seem to have some
ants crawling up your ass"
to the man at the locker
next to mine in the
changing room of
the public swimming pool

who took off his shirt
with no concern for the
line of tiny black ants
that emerged from his
right nipple and wandered
up and over his shoulder

and turning aside to
shuck his pants the ants
continued down a shoulderblade
crossed his spine
curled around one buttock
and disappeared in the crack.

"Excuse me mister" I could not say
even though I knew about tattoos
while he suited up and
went to swim and I
combed my wet hair
rolled my towel and
went the other way

for about fifty years
wondering what imagination or
intent or resolve or alcohol
created that permanent
trail of ants and by not
saying "Excuse me mister"

and asking him to
define his ants did I
miss some great teaching
or maybe even young and
stupid I sensed this was
a philosophy that I
in my blue sky summer
was not ready for.

A bicycle to ride.
A wind to dry my hair.
Good enough for now.

My Brother's Theory

As a child he carefully
reduced a clock to its parts
and in the beauty of
its entrails read the future.

Human beings were just
a necessary step in the evolution
of intelligent machines

requiring first the separation
of consciousness from
the moment being lived.
Click bzzzz what trained
my understanding of time

plugged me in to cellular
video virtual scramble?
So far so good
for the well-oiled spark.

My brother thinks
it will be a while yet
before the perfect servant
gains the keys to the house

and maybe it's just an illusion
that we continue doing our
best to be anywhere
but where we are.

Still the long shot calls.
Beneath it all in some
deep muscle of memory
the grass rolls on
the great drum beats.

After The Hunt

Once was the taking of
the buffalo with lances
then arrows then bullets.
Some of that brown river

tumbled down to
sustenance or commerce.
The rest ran away
over the hills and
out of our history.

No literature tells what followed
when our trails diverged
where they finally stopped
the calling out among themselves
finding each other.

The diminished herd
reforms itself in farewells
we may take credit for
but cannot join.

Someone might have heard
the ones that called
all night with no answer
but those ceremonies of loss
are held beyond
the light of our fires.

Ride

All the times we rode
this country highway
now I drive solo
in the wake of your coffin

though I can hear you
railing at the stupid assholes
who don't know enough to
pull over for a funeral.

Well buddy the selfish
are always with us
even as the redtail circles
passing winter wheat

takes hold in the dirt
and wild geese continue
to break our hearts somewhere
between laughter and song.

A loss of company.
A certainty of presence.
Ride with me.

Behind

It is quiet back here
behind the times

on the flat perspective of
this ground over which civilization
has already passed
I am coming behind

sayings have already been said
events have all happened
back here the evidence
of lies the world told itself
and all the obsessions
of the dead the living
found no use for

Far ahead the thin
line of horizon dust
where Things Are Happening
and all the jetsam discarded
moves around my feet

I sit on a busted suitcase
thinking a man might
make a life
among these civilized scraps . . .
gather up all these
abandoned Easter chicks . . .
start a little farm.

Kansas Night Storm

If streaming down a highway
and the window rolled up
what a shame.
That hot moist rush of
dark wants to feel you

strong sweat of weeds
in your head winding
scree of frog and insect
and black deer leaping

at the corner of your eye.
Lightning might walk
and wind might crow.
This is all yours.

Journey

Just for a moment
in the passing dark
a small window hangs
yellow with a mans

bare shoulders and head
leaning to a boy
applying lather to the
mans face with a brush

glimpses come and quickly go
rain on thin arms
a bird killed and buried
babies grin lopsided wisdom

again and always again
the tubes uncurling
into leaves greening
browning snapping free

each a brimming history
even in the
darkness that follows
the man and boy remain

a ceaseless round
preserved in the
intent of their gaze
the precise thought that
inhabits the curve of a hand

Connection

The solitary drop of cold water
having fallen so far
from summer blue skies
towering cloud.
The shirtless boy
seventeen years alive on
the hill of yellow grass

and sandstone slabs
he is turning over
in order to discover
the other side.

On a shoulderblade
flushed by sun the drop
of cold water falls
and stuns him with pleasure
into everything else.

A single strike of rain
and he is in the vibrant
family of matter
all connected and
in need of no theory.

From this touch onward
he has only to
remember to belong.

Ghost World

Starting Point

Baloney and swiss all the way
back home I thought
wheat bread and miracle whip

half past midnight
in the land where a team
of men called eagles
roll over a group
of men called saints
with over a million witnesses

but baloney and swiss the full moon
and the dogs on full wail
the wild goose flying through
that swarm of sound
could think on his mortality
all the way to mexico

elsewhere today tomatoes were thrown
at a black jaguar immune to bullets
a birdwing stuck up on the highway
slapping the breeze
and beneath the dotted line

old dadas lay laughing
the world is so crazy
I pray for home
if it please God not to
squash Thy weird servant

for surely the real mystery is
that nothing given enough rope
always becomes something?

the landscape at large
shrugged in unison said search me
wedge open the windows
let a sandwich be your starting point.

The Invention Of The Doorway

The wall came first.
People soon got tired
of taking down the rocks
going in
then putting the rocks
back up again.
A person had a thought:

what was needed was
a Hole in Matter she said.
Long after the people had
stoned her to death
they began to
consider the idea.

When it was found to work
the scariest person claimed it
and called it doorway.
This person had power but
the tribe had killed its thinker.
The door was not invented
for another five hundred years.

The Cherokee Princess Factory

it was somewhere in the south
hidden of course
before the people took
the walk to Oklahoma

they came out shining brown
red in the cheeks
long-fringed white leather
a single vertical feather

they laughed like water
moved like fawns
a hundred princesses a moon
came off the line

every mountain was a pedestal
every waterfall a backdrop
they filled the land
so full that "hold your fire boys"
invaders said "it's just
another Cherokee princess"

invaders took deserts mountains
forests and prairie ocean to ocean
and thousands of Cherokee princesses
became common currency
two of them equaling
a pound of salt

the factory was never found
though there is a plaque in a
parking lot somewhere in the carolinas
and each princess sits securely
in a pale family tree

Timeless Peasants Report

The priest had a vision
his own articulate bones
facing the sky.
Strange people on their knees
brushed and sniffed around them.

When he died it was
with a jade sphere in one hand
jade cube in the other
the bones of the hands
found kingdoms later
by the delicate lick of the brush.

Material: jade.
Configuration: one sphere one cube.
Purp: to be held in one
hand or the other.
Subpurp: dualism existential
zen matrix old stuff
the world swiftly understands
(clever savage all the same).

Timeless peasants report night chants
but the priest is dead unable
to see vision ravel on

his story continuing as one
of a series of rectangular stories
found preserved in the bogs of Earth
and deciphered with great difficulty

the wood pulp ordered
with black language marks
being randomly covered with
what proves to be parakeet excrement.
Some sort of Bird Cult is suspected.

Word of old stories about old stories
even filters back to timeless peasants
cutting peat cubes who report
invisible laughter on the bogs

and with universal shrugs
turn back to soup rice noodle bean.
These things they understand.
To someone else a vision comes
of how their world will change.

The Skunk

Wandering into the summer
barbecue with a preoccupied
foam along your lip
and not about to take
any crazy shit from anybody

that's the way it feels
to be young and mad and
restless and a skunk.

The night once carried forever that
tang of mouse on the breeze

but time has not been coy
your Identity Profile changes:
suddenly you stink and are on
everyone's hit list
cars   dogs   hunters   boys.

One burning afternoon all hope
of ever being your own skunk
snaps out.
You walk straight into town
where the fear they look for

in your eyes
begins to appear in their own.
In your brotherhood there is a thought:

He is only a hunter
who can spare a skunk.
You will fight everyone you meet.

Private Property

the chunk of butter passed
from hand to hand around
the campfire meal became
equal parts hair grease and dirt
and ran down the diners' arms

and so the butter dish
was invented the butter
could go round unhandled
but now diners chased

the butter around the plate
with their mouths until they
got a bite and passed it on
and the butter was rendered
as unattractive as before

it was then a radical
postulation was made—
butter could exist as fragments
of itself—resulting in the
invention of the butter knife

to cleave and claim
ones own butter
to dirty by oneself.

To Recognize Evil

It smells proper
and carries a speech
it has written for God.

Its praise
a decorated rope
and daily bread resentment
evil being evil

lets nothing show
just waits knowing
each has their own appointment.

When it does leap smiling
headlong from the mirror
who will deliver us?

Particle by particle
we make salvation
lined up with the
world all at once.

To know and call it
to account by name
we trust the voices
gathered in our bones.

Porches And Kitchens

Overlooking lawn or linoleum
in swirls of conversation
scarred wood in yellow light

places of liquid and smoke
where one might tell another
they were just plain wrong

sometimes there were insects
calling out or small
wings circling the light

celebration grew here
argument and philosophies
too arcane to interpret

cicadas keened promises
made and undone
behind laughter and loss
the refrigerator droned

where beings once gathered
dreams that still
hover on porch chairs and
shadow empty table tops

Howling For Dollars

Just before showtime the
smell of hot dollar grease
is snorted by the contestants.
You inhale a misery down
to the root of your neck.

The dog on a rope at night
is your master   he remembers
that something happened
but forgets it was the dark
chance of the trail.

Now into the deep green mosaic
of lenses and grids
you pull from your bones
a cry to engage gods.

If there is any pungency
of coyote or wolf
you lose.

On the video bank the faceless
public votes are coming in
the numbers piling up

judging the truth of
your lonesome regret while
far off soft feet walk
on white white sand.

In Another Life

Hitler and the nazis
take over my country
making me one of a gang
that unloads semis
of goods furniture art
appliances into a warehouse.

Knowing it must come
from citizens but not
what to do about it
in the gloomy trailer
I lay a bookend on a
marble table and light
a cigarette. The air stiffens.

Hitler walks in with
a retinue of minders
fingers a few items
asks my brand and
bums a smoke which
he lights himself
sees I want to
kill him but I
also want to live
nods twice with a
carry on flip of the hand.

Walking nowhere with others
on fringes of a dump
mangled clothes machinery
car parts mud and glass
in my offtime of a bad day
commended by Hitler
and relieved of a cigarette
I meet an old friend.

His T-shirt has a three
word design in elaborate
interlocked script which
I solve into THE LOST JEW.
My friend cautions me
to keep it to myself
and adds that he
misses New York.

We kick small bits
of slag ahead with broken shoes.
Another wanderer says to
his friend—I hope they
catch that lady who's
making her own refrigerator.
She's giving us all
a bad name—

The Lost Jew shares
a glance of grey light
and that is how the day
I could have jammed a
cigarette up Hitler's nose
into his brain ended.

Bird Master

Tipping a head with its advice
intend less and wonder more
the bird waited

for the bubble of thought in
my mind to form as
what does that mean?

It means I have no intention
to explain one spread of
delicate toes shifted

and I wonder why you ask.

At The Stoplight

Waiting at the stoplight
from a bar by the car window
a man enters sideways
the afternoon sun

coat rucked off one shoulder
necktie stripped loose and streaming back
hands before him as if
he might yet grab some
part of what's been lost

but the world he dressed for
is no longer there
face twisted red from panic to regret
he throws himself upon the
domed blue top of the
mailbox at your elbow

and into crossed arms wails
all the names of his forsaken history
the light changes
and you go on
but you only think you do.

Why You Should Read This Poem

Because it contains
no advice.

Because you're here now
somehow finding it
and completion is
its own reward.

Because it requires no
proof of purchase
ownership or identity.

Because in the
victory of excess
someone must travel
small and light.

Because it doesn't ask
you to save the world
but believes you will.

Smugglers Of Hammers

When the grandfather wished
to know when he lived
he looked at the machine
where two precision arrows circling
like earth around sun
deposited him at three
thirty in the afternoon.
Children of his children
see colored numerals.
The phenomenon goes slowly out
shadowed by its symbol.

To their children
events cease to exist
and numbers which describe them
come breathlessly real.
Then some will feed the machines
some will read them
some will be smugglers of hammers.

Moon And Shadow

the ripe moon
the streaming cloud shadows

the quaking blue
field of strawberries

creatures passed here once
and others will

pass through and through
and through this enduring

dominion of shadow and moon
the strawberries are sweet

Trouble Brewing As Hogs Near Paradise

Each night their fires
light the hills closer
to the lurid calm falling
over barricades.

The sleep of Paradise is
punctured with their cries.
Disaster is dreamed
by all but the rational
who say Paradise is
a state of mind
who say even hogs
have a creation story.

God was invited to damn hogs
by a local resident
the hogs   the hogs
it's always the hogs
said God when the
matter was presented
very well   what name
are the hogs going
by this time?

But the hogs decided
being damned was
a state of mind
and came chowing
down and spewing
out river after sky.

Like the memory of a forest
smoke columns rise
as they quench their fires
in the ultimate dawn
of Paradise.
Here they come.
We can smell their desire.

White Boys In Control

What does a white boy know?
Anything a boy of any color wants to know.
Why do so many white boys not want to know?
They do know, but they don't want to admit it.
Why don't they want to admit it?
If they admitted what all the living earth knows by
heart, they would have to forsake the desire to control.
Why do they want to control?
Greed and pride together.
Why do they have greed and pride?
Because they do not want to know.
What do they not want to know?
Respect for the harmony of life.
Why do they fear that?
It gives the power to live, but not the power to control.
Why do they want the power to control?
It is a mystery to me.
How can we change this?
We can only live what we know.
What will happen if we cannot change it?
Creation will shrug off control.
Then the end of the world is coming?
No. Don't think that way. The end of the world
is happening now.

Snooker

We shouldn't even try
snooker in a place where
televisions hang tilted from
the tops of walls
each locked soundless
on a different channel

pool maybe
with its yawning pockets
not this game so delicate
and unforgiving players
need always to address
the table or each other

but this is the world
you are coming into
distraction is cool   you might wonder
did my my my generation
take too many drugs
or not enough

sink a red ball first
one point   then a number
the tiny Sonics race the tiny Pistons
across a tiny floor
the red stays in
the numbered ball
a car a sentence
this is the car you were
born to drive
comes out to play again

when you absently track
your eyes to a screen
and call out in a shock
of bare woman legs

thrown up and back
a shiny metal rod thrusting in
and a picture then of what

is being pierced inside
I want to hold and spare you
from the quick startle
shudder and curl
but only hopeless say
don't watch that son

and level the cue to my shot
red in the side pocket
and miss the four
and pronounce nothing
and say it's your turn
as if all answers might be
found in the pursuit of making
this cluttered table clean

Ghost World

On the world window
two little people wrestle
in a tub of mustard
while those who can are
piping The Beatles 'Across the Universe'
to Polaris. It will
arrive in 431 years

when it will become noise
or bounce off rock or
wise roaches may chime
"They seem like reasonable
beings. At least it's not
a declaration of war.
Or is it? What do they
mean 'Across the Universe'?"

431 years away
a list is kept
bees bats coral frogs
of those unable
to participate in progress.
In this ghost world
the hand need not touch
but invariably wants to.
Three bald boys kickroll
a skeletal Christmas tree in

the dark outside the cab.
The cabbie pulls over.
They are desecrating
the Baby Jesus. He
pulls out his gun.
They pull out their guns.
Privilege clutches its chin.
A sparrow gets put
on the list.

Against Surrender

they are skeletons or less now
who spoke through the night
agonies of confusion at the
timeless human choice
of fear to anger to violence

before you were as much as
a slippery dream of seed
generations of lowered heads sorrowed
this self centered history
there have always been some to
champion love but never enough

those who embraced have all fallen
to dust and memory and those who
attacked fallen to dust and memory
all are falling still around you where
you weep at the prison power builds

so it has always seemed hopeless
your tiny moment guarantees
no worth to gestures of grace
you must make them anyway
though the bones blow away
the right butterfly

lands on the wrong tree
and skies heave with regret
your small offerings
counter monuments to self
beyond vision reason or might

Living To Tell About It

In a bare dirt field
windstream takes the small
hawk feather from my hat

Shall I chase thee?

Walking with clouds
learning to smell like a weed
the evening news is
sixteen chips of flint

a wren crossing over
the field yesterday
had fallen and died.

The sun goes pink
behind spheres of grain.
The farmer titles his field
The Best Stand Of
Milo On The Planet.

Black highway feather
in my truck cab rattles.
Full moon
surrounded with blue dust
could be a movie in my windshield
if I were an idiot and it
not the full moon
surrounded with blue dust.

The whole valley plowed
dark for rain.
On the passenger seat
a cantaloupe   a memory of vines
a breath sweet and rank.

Just Before Midnight

just before midnight
small and old
the man appears on
his quiet porch
sweeps it clean while
snow still falls sweeps
one foot slowly in
front of the other
the long sidewalk
a step and the double
swish of broom
unhurried and even
out to the curb where
he stops to lean into
the soft wet
dance of snow
silent in the
sleep of others
the spring of the broom
breathing his moment
on this new
path in the night

Being New

Being new to this storm of sensations
you just begin to gather sense
and here comes a path
through the stars.
Being here dear pilgrim

is more than being
told who to be
yet we tender these crude
signs to your map.
Learn the names and remember

they are only names.
Should your edges blur
turn to the moment
praise the different sky
you are given each day.

May fire only comfort
water bear you up
stone be gentle and the air
of falcons tend your passage.
Welcome small traveler

your journey defines our joy.
We belong to you now.

Preparing To Leap To The Moon

We will be leaping through
the outer spheres of the earth
and traveling light.

First we take a good
look at the moon

not charts and maps
I mean that little pokerface
way the hell off.

Now we have a good laugh
since our task is
clearly impossible.
Now we prepare.

Our legs and brains hum
hard and blue.
We leave a tangle on the air
the sound of trailing laughter.

Dirt

An infinite component
of existence according
to the housewifes lament
our planet calls its
name in gentle synonym
while we spend a life

trying to keep it off us
sweep dust mop
washing all our objects
temporarily clean and
there is no dog lie bastard
worse than a dirty one.

Beneath our contempt
dirt continues.
All the dirt that left
grand canyons behind
the ghosts of mountains
crawl speck by mote
to the seas

and all that is not dirt
quietly on its way
the disintegrating leaf
before the forest
as the crumbling brick
foreshadows cities.

Dirts dominion
takes its certain time.
Our ageless companion
the dirt of stars
informs the hand
a kinship best

expressed alone
grasping and letting it
fall between fingers.
Yes. This will do
just fine.

Speak Now

speak now your
animal voice brother
understand blood
possess childhood
scream a long blind night
the breath that runs dark
with hope and wounded music

speak for the other
even after there is
no more to be said
after all the shoes
of the dead have been gathered
sing beyond ashes

Harley Elliott lives in Salina, Kansas.

Other publications by him include DARKNESS AT EACH ELBOW and ANIMALS THAT STAND IN DREAMS (both poetry) from Hanging Loose Press, Brooklyn, NY and THE MONKEY OF MULBERRY PASS (poetry) and LOADING THE STONE (non-fiction) from Woodley Press, Topeka, KS.